Also by Sam Hamill:

Heroes of the Teton Mythos

Uintah Blue

Petroglyphs

forthcoming:

Triada

The Calling Across Forever

THE CALLING

ACROSS FOREVER

SAM HAMILL

COPPER CANYON PRESS
PORT TOWNSEND

Thanks to the editors of the following
publications in which some of these poems
initially appeared: *Blue Moon News,
Cincinnati Poetry Review, dalmo'ma,
Emphasis, Los, Marilyn, Paintbrush, Portland
Review, Gravida, Montana Gothic.*

NOTE:
The Loom I-V appears in *PETROGLYPHS*
(Three Rivers Press, Box 21, Carnegie-Mellon
University, Pittsburgh, Pennsylvania 15213).

Special thanks to Jo Cochran; Patti Pattee
and Bill O'Daly; *Centrum Foundation*, Port
Townsend, Washington, where Copper
Canyon is Press-in-Residence; and for a grant
which in part made possible publication of
this book, the National Endowment for the
Arts, a federal agency.

ISBN 0-914742-23-X

Copper Canyon Press
P.O. Box 271
Port Townsend, Washington 98368

For Kathy Ransom

"What matters is the quality *of affection."* —*E.P.*

CONTENTS

Selected Letters

LETTER TO MY ELDERLY FATHER

No stars burn above that burning western city.
Far overhead that "silver sliver of a moon"
is pocketed in clouds. September.
The cottonwoods will once again be bare.
The slow traffic crowding through the streets
will pass the house you built and no more own.
Your protesting child has long since gone,
is quiet as a tomb. That gold trumpeting angel
will see to your city now. California,
Colorado, and now the Puget Sound.
I couldn't breathe in that damnable town.
When I walk beside the grey flat water
and old gulls shriek and dive,
I curl my lips, but cannot wholly smile.
One divided among one, I squint down all those years.
It's like looking at the sun.

The mosquitoes here
are smaller than on Black Rock Beach
in the swelter of those years. Instead of slag
and fuming smelter, there's a paper mill
burns poison into air. What you wanted for me then
was somehow always wrong. Say I'm still
your wayward boy, out for a coastal lark,
say I drink too much and smoke too much,
still too careless where I walk. Say
only our shadows are long. Say I've nine grey hairs
nestled in my beard, that I'm still the stubborn fool
writing poems in the dark.

X: 75

LETTER TO RANSOM IN UTAH
with snapshots from Black Rock Beach

Was here, sweating on that filthy beach
with a girl whose name and face escape me
I first saw that dead lake ironic,
Antelope Island bare in the saltwater wake.
Here, a crusty old Black Rock with rusty iron pipe
to grip as you climb it.
The view from there was never very much.
Even late at night the sand was always warm
and cracked like frozen snow beneath our feet.
Down that road the City of Salt, like Sodom,
stood stripped in neon and defeat.
Searchlights illuminate Moroni's golden horn.

And here, as if to scorn, they pour magma
molten down the hill. Its incandescent glow
throws fire on the water and fear
like a giant lizard dozes in the chill.
Down this road a neighbor boy hatcheted
two girls who refused to change his tire.
We shotgunned rabbits from the back
of his hotwired pickup truck. Turds
and tourists bathed in Jordan River.
Was it here the saintly gulls
spewed locusts and returned? Listen,
the ore-car's on the track again.
That hole called Bingham
was once a mountain, friend.

X:75

12

TO A CHILDHOOD SWEETHEART

Always, there was the setting forth.
Where we lay smoldering in fields
watching geese rise slowly through a mist
the vague hills rose one behind another
marching toward clouds like conquistadors.
We found those linings not silver,
but hard, ice-bitten steel.

And now we shift in the night,
a continent between us,
and remember low light, clouds,
a summer we wore like a gown,
naked aspen simmering over the hill,
and the one stark note of our bodies
vibrato in the air.

XII: 75

LETTER TO QUIGLEY
from the Quimper Peninsula

To you, in New York City now,
the water birds were myth.
But let me talk of the wind.
A man could squander his whole life
remembering what he loved.
Those shrill birds plunge into the water
and rise again renewed. A wife
is a leaky boat, at best, a way
to wander till the tide comes in.
Choked in those dingy streets you'll recall
how the fog out here
turns all the sunsets amber,
how the pitted tracks run parallel
onto the rotting dock. Barbwire
crosses them up the hill
where bunch grass obliterates the ties.
After the trains, some cattle I'd guess,
but none now, nor anyone to herd them.
This broken town breaks no one any more.
It's dead winter and winter mist
pours all the sunsets bourbon.

I: 76

14

DEAR TREE,

I have been walking the graveyard
in a strange town. The few stiff leaves
break softly under my heels
while I read *Albertson, Madison, Coles,*
with the wind reminding my bones
I'm still alive. My lives
have taken to darkness like eels
rubbing the cool bottom gravel
where the thinnest currents dwell.
What are these February birds,
these dry streets in Idaho,
what do I know? The night
has plunged into my eyes
and no two streets sing the same.
There is no rehearsal for the highway.

Yet there is music:
that the dead sang to Roethke in his sleep,
that Berryman wept,
that Hugo still enflames.
I, too, blaze with hope, and I'm not ashamed
to say I love you in a poem,
although, forgive me,
it is hard to say it well.
We are strange as these graves
of strangers, just as temporary here,
and just as given over
to the passions, monstrous and lovely,
of our lives. We are lost
in the graveyards of lost cities
where only the music survives.

21:II:76

15

NIGHTLETTER TO SISTER LORRAINE

Curled in a narrow room, low light
falling in the sadness of music,
I sit and smoke, thinking the river.
Is that the Snake, is that where I am?
Strong winds intimidate this valley
pushing the moon away.
You've heard that moan, I'm sure.
This odd, arthritic town
somehow keeps on breathing,
its roily water
keeps the old heart beating.
A mill disguised near Lewiston
conspires against the air.
Up the hill the Orchards,
fast food and easy beer,
where big beeves munch slowly
the late winter stubble
or relieve old itch
against a sagging fence
while a single bison poses,
disdainful on the crest.

Ugly skies scowl down
on the rubble of Culdesac.
You've seen them all before.
And there's nothing in Sunday papers,
churches and Birchers
buying the biggest ads,
and taverns do roaring business.
Don't get me wrong, these
are damned fine folks right here,
the stock that made this land.
But the money's all been made
and moved to more prosperous climate.
There's work and weather written here,
no time for serious despair
unless that river strangles.
And though the rigs roll through without stopping
and the world goes ornery on its way,
Lewiston, under a granite rim,
gets through another day.

II: 76

LETTER TO RANSOM IN RAYMOND

Jesus, Bill, what keeps them here,
these obdurate shacks and wracked barns
bleeding through their stains?
This evening, coming home,
there were cows on the road again.
Where fields are tilled lies a stain
colored tobacco-riddled lung
in which lie pools like spat-out phlegm.
Where there is grass, even grass
is gray. At the threshold of despair
they sleep, dreaming immaculate defeat.

I sit at my table and smoke.
How are things in Raymond. Tell me
a joke. There are more birds returned
every day, it must be spring.
Soon, the bright light low
burning the fields quartz, thin shoots
blushing green from pale. Must be
hard work getting old. Sometimes I think
we've sold ourselves in hell.

A dog yowls from the mill. Not a star.
The sky's a ceiling even a midget
could stuff a fist through.
Whatever it's like where you are,
the homestead's just the same,
sea and sky beleaguered gray,
no blue. But we stay in the tatters
of our labor, the shards of our hope.
Seems there's always a friend coming home
from somewhere down the road.

17:III:76

18

LETTER TO MY DAUGHTER

When April snarls belligerent to its end
eaves in the old barn complain, smoke
lurches from the chimney, disappears
wandering down the waterway. Snowy mountains
sink down south into a rising tide
of green, and lost on a high plateau,
old friends are planting trees. Yesterday
the clouds were horsetails switching
in the breeze. Today a dark like solstice
promises rain. Crows hunch up
in low boughs of the orchard, shadows
of the herd grow pale. The hammered
pewter sky shuts down the field, closes
the kelp beds where the sand sharks feed,
bleeding through foxtail and thistlejack
and scotchbroom blooming near the swamp.

The heart throbs like the bowman's arrows
eager in the quiver when the first
roll of thunder drums across the ear.
A drop, then two, streak the dirty window.
I have tried to read the sky, only to fall
sprawling on my face when a snagged toe
betrayed pretension. Not stars, nor heaven guide us.
Lost between answer and question, between
tide and tide, weather and weather,
we look both ways down a highway,
don't cross it, but walk it.
A thousand miles divide us. But rain
and clouds are one, the sun is the same.
When wind drives rain against your sleep
be still. We are together & the road
shows the way to our feet.

IV: 76

19

LETTER TO HUGO

They'd put a pox on you, Poor Richard,
and damn me if I wouldn't go along.
An NBA nominee. And the second time around.
What can they know in New Yawk City,
what can it mean in the end? Cracked drunks
stand in Missoula doorways
waving out at the rotund man
guiding the flip-top Buick
with shades on his balding pate.
These are the highways that were his eyes.
Pithy bastard, they'll say, and
he's earned his weight in bourbon.
Sometimes spring run-off
begins at the mouth. You've heard them
explain away their hair or dive
into a glass; one foot on the gas
and the open road ahead, you left them
far behind in the dust.

Critics go stone mad
drinking what their subjects drank.
Marlowe died on a barroom floor and lay there
till he stank. For What? Forty years
you recorded what you drank. Miles and heat
from the sand bars, tugs, bridges and defeat
you remember cormorants and grebes, the names
of certain streets, but where you went
from there you somehow remember wrong.
After all, you've a wife, a family now.
I, for one, can't figure why critics bother.

As Kung once said to a few disciples,
each man answers correctly, that is, each
in his own manner. And this
of course without adding
some men better than others. They'd
promise you the stars, but they
can't put them in your hand.
I look to the past for you
where bars were always bars and sad
until you shed that solemn light
standing eyeball to eyeball with the sun
till you stared that darkness down.
What's true rings true. Be pleased.
When the mobs acclaim a loner,
it diseases. Out of the dark of those poems,
forward steadily as songs of loss whirling
from a Wurlitzer, moves that ideogram,
the pictograph of integrity, a shape
not seen, but heard: "a man
standing beside his word."

IV: 76

LETTER TO HEDIN

My Grampa was short and thick and German.
His pock-scarred bulbous nose
usually filled with RoiTan smoke.
What fingers he had were mostly stub
and souvenirs of mines. I remember
how rarely he spoke, how strong
he was, broad shoulders and a monk's
straight-as-an-arrow back. He inhabited
an old man's hotel with a lobby
solemn as a mortuary. I rarely went there
and never to his room. I remember him
among the flags and snap-dragons
shovelling manure in Ma's old garden.

I write you this not because
you'd have liked him (you would), but
because we are poets; it is for us
to remember and define. You
who are lean and tall
are like him: quiet, observant,
and intent. All the works and days
of hands with ten full fingers
are at your command. We who have
everything have less: we cuss the silence
and the silence blesses us.

What odd hotels will hold us
when we are old and bones?
In what second-rate retreat
will we learn to lick our wounds
when the roses of desire wither in our skins
and that old friend agility
is evicted from our feet. Can we,
you and I, endure those small, untimely
every-day defeats that old age visits
with earnest, absolute regularity?

Writing this to you,
I'm feeling old already, old enough
for foreign towns and hand-me-down hotels,
thankful for a home-cooked meal,
a letter now and then. True
to the craft to the end, nothing
counterfeit or cruel, thankful
to be living and for a few
wily and durable friends.

14:IV:76

LETTER TO O'DALY

We thought the day would never end.
As we stood at the dusty summit
overlooking the tide, the green sea
far beneath our feet, we thought
the dark would never come, that scrub pine
and sunshine was all there was to see.

One afternoon on the boulder
with the highway curving off below
was an eternity back then.
Diesel smoke and weed
was a maniac perfume. San Marcos Pass.
I disremember years. Slow,
winding the old truck up
where foxtail browned beside the road,
a hundred years ago.

And Denver. Where'd it go.
You'd think we'd tire, or that
we'd've found what we're looking for.
Xrist, I talk like I'm getting old.
Daylight and darkness keep moving,
moving on. If we burn with the fire
that consumes, it's a pleasure.
Cheers. What-the-hell.

IV: 76

LETTER FROM THE PIONEER BAR & GRILL

Each day I crawl the tattered edge of town
near the wasted boats and scattered hopes
of last year's bankrupt trollers.
Low wind drives a sea-scent down the street
weaving little in-tide waves
into a shimmering finger wandering naked
through the pebbles on the beach.
Up concrete steps and through
a heavy wooden door, you'll find me
seated at the bar. Two stools down
a native grey as Sitka weather
rocks atop his stool. Eddie the barkeep smiles
and brings a bourbon down. It's friendly here
and quiet; the bars stay open late.

"No dogs allowed" the sign says on the door,
and judging from the downtown whores
and big red dog asleep behind the bar,
that rule's interpreted at will.
The local parts man drinks here
and bought us all a round; the regulars
are few, but regular as hell. The mirror's
uncracked for a change, and above it
a fleet of beached, reefed, and sundered craft
hangs in dimestore frames. Hag and Waylon
monopolize the box, and there's some
gentle rock'n'roll, the kind you hear
the clack, clack of pool balls through.

"Alcoholic" you said. Matter of fact.
And if it's true, it's dead reckoning
got me here. The foreign air and thick
sodden days appeal. I don't apologize.
I like my liquor with a beer, my music
melancholy slow, and elbow workday grimy.
The ancient violence subsides. My eyes
have seen a world a kind heart revises.
My bum leg drags behind like the ghost
of an evil past. No matter, friend,
the fury of an angry world. Good will
persists in a friendly bar if bars
are where you live. May northern tides
enthrall you, the old rain reassure.
Yours in this old world
from the Pioneer Bar & Grill.

29:VII:76

LETTER FROM KETCHIKAN

for the Kotlarovs

At the sultry, torpid dock a tourist boat,
Cunard, pumps blue diesel smoke
into a breezeless day. Slacktide
and the hundred gift shops overflow.
Fishing's closed since a week ago
and the marina reeks anger and despair.
The stolid Ketchikan Public Library
houses a museum. Call it big creek
or small river, depending
on where you came here from,
it races beneath our window
over jutted mossy rocks,
all whitewater and pretty
enough to use in our poems. They
even stock some poetry here,
though mostly from the dead.
Where I stay is up a mile of hill
and eighty wooden steps then up
a flight inside. Out my window
above the handsome bay, spruce-laden
mountains harbor a little snow.
In forty bars downtown
haggard faces waste another day.
Soon, the EPA
is closing the pulp mill down.
With no mill, no fish in the sea,
and September coming on, it's
no damn wonder some men wear
a tacky streak of mean.
As for me, I'm doing fine,
if anyone should ask you. Just say
I'm doing fine for an old young man
in Kiss My Axe, Alaska.

2:VIII:76

TO DAVIA, ALONE

Down Tongass Narrows,
above the low lip of fog,
an eagle scarred by a hundred
ravens' claws limps homeward
in the rain. Below,
a Tlingit elder lifts
his paddle from the wave.
Down the polluted beach,
among tin cans submerged in rust,
among bones of halibut and cod,
beached and smelling bad,
old kelp decays.

Alone in your shack south of town,
you gaze out
across the flat grey water.
Out back a black bear
shuffles leisurely
through your garbage.
You remember a garland of yarrow
someone wove once for your hair,
how your hair
smelled of yarrow for hours.

On this decaying coast we thrive alone.
Alone in life we learn
to die alone. Learn to make
laughter from beach scrap, joy
from spat out bones.
Curled at night in your blanket,
remember this
when nightmare rips your sleep:
above the shivering trees old stars
rain down a thousand kisses.

10:VIII:76

28

Postcards & Petroglyphs

THE CALLING ACROSS FOREVER

Turning again to the sea, the immense
and female sea, I search the naked cliff
raw and alone above the strait and with wind
enough for a chill; steadily, the rain
recites the tears I might have sung
to these high groves of cedar and fir
while through sheer clouds and rain the sunset
pours blood across the sea, last embers
of burning daylight throbbing in the breeze
in ripples on the water. The salt of blood
thickens my tongue. From islands
undefined in the hemispheres of the brain
the sirens sing, their calling
calling across rocks and mosses
in a soft flopping of wings uplifting
the jaundiced eye and frozen hands into
a hunger, a dry mouth that cannot sing.

What
have I come to? I have felt tides
urging at my loins, the pale wings of the moon
driving its beak to the marrow. Tomorrow,
in an hour of frenzy an impassioned coho
will smash its crimson flesh to bits
against the stones of a shallow pool.
Is it that old heron Fear
props me one-legged and watching,
shoulders hunched up for the dive
across the calling of forever, the blood
scrambling over the edge into the pure air
of knowing
above the tide-torn rocks below?

In this falling off of light, this
cadence of desire caught in the sea-surge,
the heart clasps its bone cage and thunders,
rage boils in the blood like oil, an ancient
shudder grips the spine
rattling loose the split halves of the tongue.
A raven reels over the sea.
His one anguished cry
spills over the earth piercing
the lost desolate waste places of the mind
where the saddest of dreams are hoped.
The sea and the psyche flame, burn.
I kneel, kissing the smoke.

The sea paints white
the narrow strip of sand
along the shallow beach beneath my feet.
The white moons of her nails, electric,
wander across my skin. I listen in the dark:
erratic candlefish
swarm through the inlet near the reef,
sharks doze
half-submerged in sand, the sea sighs
rolling her belly, breathing. Asleep
at her side I thirst for Paradise,
a glimpse from the high
heaven Icarus glimpsed before he fell
human and male to the sea. I, too,
would drown, happily drown
in the seas of a muse's eyes, anguished
as any raven, lemming mad, shivering frenzy,
loved, dying, but alive.

1-10: V: 76

32

LEARNING TO SWIM

In a pre-dawn glow we lay
hugging our bones for worth.
The out-tide withdrew from the stones
leaving a small blue crab
writhing in dry air. Our mouths
were the mouths of fishes
loosing great zeroes in the tide-flow.

Down the log-strewn southern beach
the pulp mill roared to life.
Salmon berries colored like the sun
burst ripe upon the day. Tlingit women
sobbed among the wreckage of their shacks,
their naked children
turning restless in their sleep.

I dream dancing calves gleaming
on handsome women in my sleep.
Over rolling hills of memory
they dance away like fog
burned white in the sun's first heat.
The long, level lapping of the waves
repeats a sad refrain.

Bruised to irony, the wind
wanders the seamy side of town.
The depths we dive are real
for all their poverty—like salmon
against the current, blurred
by stolen silt. Leaping, I gasp,
and dawn is a gaff in my side.

INHERITING SITKA ALASKA

The pleasure craft *Jennifer*
rolls heavy in Crescent Harbor,
sleepy again today, warm sun
breaking over her bow
to burn off the morning mist.
Wandering from campus toward town,
past handsome stone Episcopal Church
with its promise of eternity,
I stumble across the old clapboard
faded Russian Mission Orphanage
easing into ruin, the old
haphazard foundation settling
into obscure angles, plywood
nailed safely over shards of window pane,
wooden steps in disarray
among foxtail, fireweed, and fern.
Torn into life from need,
it crumbles slowly now,
a reminding relic of where
those unwanted children lived.
That plastic sheet
stapled tightly to its side
must hide an ugly scar.
The boys who starved inside those walls
are grandfatherly or dead,
and the children of their angry sons
are orphaned every one.

A HARD DAY IN SITKA

Sparse sunlight
gathers the limbs of ancient spruce
beyond my rain-streaked window.
Dormant waves peruse
the pulpy islands, horizon
sinking to a blur.

In this land without night,
in this land without daylight,
pitched shivering on the shore,
I learn the witchery of centuries
curling through the blood.

Facing the frozen west,
the immense sadness of the sea,
islands rise like breasts,
like buttocks, casual knees,
of a woman poorly loved,
from whom I turned away.

ANOTHER YEAR

The year comes to us from nowhere,
from under the frosty granite
and glacial peaks of the Northern Gate
where numb, green-limbed trees
stutter in the wind. See, there,
a stubborn raven in the rain,
braving the icy fists.
Across the water a little dory
is slowly rowing in.

Last night I dreamed Tu Fu's little boat
wandering the Great River, heavy
with absence, petals, and poetry.

Owls and clouds weave witchcraft
into the slanting dusk. A lone
bittern cries across the sea
and the grey sea seethes with winter,
waves sliding forward,
the slick sea-hide sewn
with ivory loam.

Deep in the north the glittering Dipper
scoops its frosty brew where a slow train
fills failing tracks of light
drifting toward the sea. There are faces
pressed against the windows.
Again the bittern calls, its sharp note
ringing like a name.

Ribbons of water and steel touch the sea
and the sea shifts on its haunches.

ANOTHER YEAR

Dazed by clouds thick as mud, by
bare trees and squalls from the west,
at dawn I fight rain to the river
like Tu Fu on the P'eng-ya Road
fleeing the rebels, a round of months
behind me like empty bottles.

What moves in icy shallows
moves slow in heavy shadows.
Life is made not from speed, but from muscle.
Who moves has no time for sorrow.
Rain or freeze, I and the days
and the clouds in the wind go home.

Little flower cupping rain,
you are early this year
and my friend who planted you
is not here. Little gate
of pleasant dew with arms
upraised to the rain,
little red-lipped queen
or king of nothing but the rain,
detain your smile until
the hands that planted you
come home again. And then
smile wetly in the rain,
lips parted, through which
heaven's gate is seen.

FISH SERMON

for Joe Wheeler

"These straits," you said,
"can be treacherous
as any northern water."
We slipped down that canal.
Juan de Fuca lay flat
as a palm-worn silver dollar.
To the west lay kelp beds
and sand sharks: dull trouble.
Above, dark felt clouds bent close
as any Christian knelt in prayer.
Sunday. In my old homeland,
sermons of hereafter, brimstone
and tithe. But here, with friends,
tide-trolling, we tend
the fires of the living.

X: 75

POSTCARD TO KENNETH REXROTH

The maple leaves are always green up here,
and the waters of the Sound
always blue. I have been thinking
of you all day, at least
since breezes pushed the rain away
and sunshine burned the fog.
Even now, late afternoon, the coves
of Indian and Marrowstone islands
seem to steam. A small figure
slowly rows the water stopping
here and there at crab pots in the bay.
In hills unfolding away
from the sleepy little town,
fine old cedars nod in the easy wind
like the kite above the grammar school,
like grand old men.

17:IX:76

POSTCARD TO TREE
from Lewiston

Bones here masquerade as trees,
hail
snaps at the window, and the whole
of downtown Lewiston
is façade, a cool
putty cadaver.

Thunder
rolls into the valley like history.
Orange bolts crack, bleeding into cloud
as the sodden street shudders.

What lives in this skin
is eclipsed: I awaken
away from you again.

16:II:76

EVERGREEN JUNIOR HIGH SCHOOL AGAIN

The dates have all been changed, the faces
rearranged, but nothing else is new.
The kind girl with braces on her teeth
is trotting out a poem. Behind her,
a brawny boy dreams home, swears he's found
a girl he can love, but blushes at her name.
Two girls lean against the wall
exchanging notes from math. They dream
of Miss America. Their dreams are sad.

I wrench a name from down my mind
and wonder if her daughter's here.
Twenty years can blind. I search these rooms
for what I may have left behind, a mark, a scar
across an upstairs wall, a battered locker door.
Nothing changes, yet everything is more.
Are those the same tough boys
brawling in the snow? The busted lip goes down.
A bloody nose has won. Triumph is adoring eyes
and blood smeared lightly on a sleeve.

Nights in strange rooms you wonder why you came.
You pop a seventh beer, sneering
at that stranger in the mirror. You fool
yourself again. A bell rings softly
in your ear. The class walks out.
Nothing changes. Nothing is the same.

3:III:76

AT TOM'S PLACE, AT TWILIGHT,

                                        the evening sighs
            in the cedar grove, the pond mirrors
            the wings of darting swallows and sailing clouds,
            and new shoots of grass nip the ground
            along the edge of a path
            leading past the house, past
            the sweathouse on its stilts, curling gently
            toward the wood; and the chickens
            exit the run for the hen-house, leisurely,
            with the old rooster in the lead,
            and the first frog of twilight
            ribbits in the reeds, and in the pole-house
            the lamps are lit with a whiff of kerosene;
            when a little wind arrives
            the old tin gate to the pasture
            rattles on its hinge.

            And the dirt road leads up from there
            over the crest of the hill
            through low boughs a mile or so
            down to a half-paved two-lane country road
            winding patiently through a valley.

                envoi
            Far from the highway and incoming tide,
            cresting on ribbons of incense and sweet red wine,
            we lightly close our eyes and listen
            for the kingfisher's three-pronged cry.

LOWEST HADLOCK, WITH FRIENDS

For J. W.

I sat in that dull shack
spat on the slackwater shore
staring out a cracked window
at nothing on the beach.
Thawing on bourbon and woodstove,
I sat watching nothing at all.
A woman roamed the few rooms in silence,
a babe in her belly,
just starting to show.
The tide creaked in.
Scrap from the mill up the beach
half-floated, foamed.
The grey beach reached the grey water
just as before.
A pick-up rattled by.
The chuck-holed, mud-holed street
died in a thousand feet.
A clip-tailed cat
curled softly at my feet.

III: 76

THAT DREAM AGAIN

Years from now
I lie among riotous springs
in that falling down hotel
in the strange seaport
where rain never stops
and no one speaks my tongue.
A lame dog curls on the dock.
Shards of faith unzip these veins
and a freighter aches in the harbor.
In a room reeking fish and sewage
I sweat into that dream
and silently mouth her name.

THE BURNING OF THE IDAHO HOTEL

"Was anyone in there when it burned?"

One old man with borrowed shoes
hunched in a sagging bed.
Probably a cigarette.
He died.
But charred brick and burnt-out beams
have memorized his name.

The kosher deli on the street
extracted his final dollar
for creamed cheese on a bagel.
Cruelty was his bride.
They honeymooned in greasy rooms,
she taught him how to beg.
She was with him to the end.

The poor saloons with smoky mirrors
all carried his brand of wine.
The drunk out back heaving up his guts
had called him his dearest friend
and hugged him for all his pain.

And now he's dead, god damn him,
in the ashes of his bed.
And when they washed him
from that gutted shell
they gave him no last name.

GIFTS

I send you this smile for the morning.
I have fallen into my mouth.
I scatter these thousand kisses
across the wind that of the thousand
wasted, one may find you and survive.

I send you these hands.
Though fingers remain warm
they hold the eternal nothing.

I send you my ears in which
words rang as gold but in which
silence forged habitat.

My eyes I keep to myself.
They have seen hunger before me
stretch out like a road
which they follow.

The Loom VI-XI

VI

From the whipped, storm-crashed inlet
salting the township mottled
to the lashed Olympics, immensely blue,
the hard squall pushes clouds around.
Where there are boats, hatches
are battened, and little hilltowns
tossed up on clear-cut slopes
catch all the hell of weather.
The swamped fields thick with calving cows
lie plundered, rubbed raw, winds
and cattle tilting fences
to strip a thicket's edges. Shaggy horses
aim their rumps up wind. No mercy
for a gull caught in cliffdraft.
Night settles like a panicked leviathan,
diving, rolling seaward.

A shingle from the mill next door
ricochets through black alder fingers.
Lamplight wavering in my narrow room
draws the ancient spatters of rain
across the rattling window. A woman
lies reading on the bed. The fire dies.
A spider bravely spins its web
across a darkened corner, traversing,
anticipating light and better weather.

VII

And if it's a calm
follows hard on the heels of the tempest,
morning finds the dark trees
gathering fingers of sunlight through leaf-buds,
dark wet earth
swearing allegiance to salal, blackberry,
and tall grasses waltzing near the swamp—
reeds form a harp
only the breeze can play.

VIII

Dogs bark along the river, a great
red-tail hawk weaves across the meadow.
What's a painter, can't read the words
of a cavedweller, what fish
thrashes on a hook in the pond?
From a crystalline sky
the sun bleeds into nettle
spreading her scarlet tunic. The breeze
stalks the reeds and the reeds quiver.

IX

I walked beside the sea
when it lay still as a sleeping woman,
little tidepools beneath my feet
and the sand free at their bottom,
and teals poured from the currents, grebes
staggered in the sun-lit reeds.

And I stood amazed
before the light white waves
lapping the feet of the town
like the sea was a dog, house-broke
and happy. A tug tooted off
near Admiralty Head where rip-tides
run regular and cruel. Another,
with barges, turned down the canal
toward Ludlow.

And a gull hopped one-footed
down the length of a beach-bleached log
chuckling only to himself. His battered wings
and chipped beak
he wore like a battle-scar.

Say it's spring, near gillnetter season,
make the tuna boat repair, do
whatever you have to to be there
before the oilport fills PA
and the green cut down
dissolves the hills
in hues of mucus gray:

Warrior Gull,
Kamikaze Teal,
despair.

X

Halcyon days, quarter past winter solstice,
neither spring nor summer, thinking now
of how the flat sheen of the water
draws cormorants to the tower
bleached and decaying in thirty feet
of water off the point. Good jigging
for cod, they'd said, but we caught nothing,
disappointing, but the sweet smoke
and sunshine across my back. On the bank
a little boy drags his line by hand,
no reel no pole. He waves his arms
and shouts. We wave an answer back.

XI

> . . . hard
in a life to know
warp from woof, threads crossing,
recrossing, the fine line of texture
weaving into pattern.

A russet sun
> shines through the clouds' veneer.
Pausing in the sleepy downtown street,
three tourists admire the maid of the fountain
spewing water in the park. The afternoon
traces cool fingers 'neath their ears,
putting little hairs on end. They buy
old brass, totemic masks, or Victorian
dinnerware. Amazed, they touch raw wool
woven to a shawl. A gull's-cry
brings a shiver, a ferry horn excites.

And in wave after little wave
the bright shells wetly shine
among the rubble on the shore.

1500 copies, designed by Sam Hamill and
Tree Swenson and printed for Copper Canyon
Press by John Laursen at Press-22 in Portland,
have been sewn into wrappers. The text is
Sonata, with Linweave Early American cover.
The type is Journal Roman with Baskerville
italic display. Fifty copies have been bound in
cloth over boards and signed by the poet. The
illustration is by Tree Swenson, after Hokusai.